The Secret Shoemakers

'WELL, my dear,' said old Gregory the shoemaker to his wife Joan, 'that's the end of the leather. I've cut out my last pair of shoes, and I'll sew them in the morning. Now I'll go to bed for I'm tired.'

'What shall we do then?' asked Joan anxiously. 'Have you nothing to buy more leather with?'

'You know we've no money for leather.'

'Can't you borrow some leather from a brother shoemaker?'

'I've borrowed all I can. Times are bad. Leather's too dear. It's all being bought to make saddles and bridles for horses to take men to the war. I'm not a saddler. I'm too old to learn a new trade. I daresay we'll get along by a bit of mending and cobbling. It's no good worrying. I'm off to bed.'

But Gregory and Joan were both worried. They had little enough to live on, nothing for new clothes, and soon the winter would be upon them and they would have to buy wood for the stove. Gregory was a fine cobbler, one of the best, but he had lost trade through a long illness. People had gone elsewhere for new shoes. Still, the old shoemaker was not one to complain about what couldn't be helped. He laid out the leather pieces on his bench in the workshop, ready to be stitched in the morning, and soon he was fast asleep in the little attic bedroom.

Next morning Gregory was amazed to find on his work bench, not a pile of leather pieces but a pair of shoes, quite finished and perfectly stitched together with neat, regular stitches.

He called his wife, and together they looked at the shoes in astonishment.

'We've got secret helpers,' said the shoemaker. 'There's no doubt of it. I couldn't do work like that in a whole week, let alone one night.'

As soon as the shop was open, customers began to come in for shoes they had left to be mended. Then towards midday a fine lady came in with her maid. She needed a pair of shoes. She could not wait to have them made to measure, as she was going on a journey that very day. Great was her delight when she found that the new shoes fitted perfectly. She was so pleased with the fine workmanship that she gave Gregory over and above what he asked for them. She had been an old customer before his illness and she knew that times were bad.

With the money she paid, Gregory hurried off to the dealer and bought enough leather for two new pairs of shoes. He gave Joan the money that was left over to buy food.

That evening he cut out two more pairs of shoes and put the pieces on the bench before going to bed. He was quite ready to begin stitching them in the morning, for he hardly dared to hope that his secret helpers would come a second night.

But sure enough, as soon as the shoemaker came downstairs in the morning, he found two pairs of finished shoes on his bench, as finely and perfectly stitched as the first pair. He was not long in finding customers for these new pairs, and with the money he got for them he was able to buy leather for four fresh pairs. With his usual skill he cut them out and left the pieces on his bench to be stitched together next day. But once more Gregory and Joan were overjoyed to find the finished shoes placed neatly on the bench next morning.

So it went on. Each night the shoemaker left a number of pairs of shoes ready to be stitched together by his secret friends, and every morning he found them finished and ready to be sold. Gregory and his wife began to be prosperous and to live comfortably as they had done in the old days. Joan had a new winter dress, and there was plenty of good dry wood to keep them warm. At last Joan said to her husband, 'Gregory, I have a mind to see who it is that helps us in the night.'

'Better leave well alone,' said her husband, though, truth to tell, he too had been wondering.

'Perhaps there is something we could do to repay them,' answered his wife. 'They may be in need of something.'

'My dear, you are right. Tonight let us leave a candle alight in the workshop and hide behind those old clothes that hang against the wall. Then we shall get to the bottom of this mystery.'

And so they did. Gregory and Joan sat on a bench against the wall, peeping out between the folds of the clothes that hid them from sight. For a long time nothing happened. At last they heard the chimes of midnight sound sleepily through the cold night air. A moment later, as if from nowhere, and with scarcely a rustle, appeared two little men. Without a word to each other they hopped on to the shoemaker's bench, sat down cross-legged, took up the leather pieces, needle and thread, and began stitching away. Never had Gregory seen such nimble fingers. The needles flashed like sparks in the candlelight, and the thread flew in and out, in and out, as if by magic.

Indeed, the little men must certainly have had magical power, for no human being could work so fast and so finely.

The shoemaker and his wife scarcely breathed, for they did not wish to scare the little men. But they noticed

that these two secret shoemakers were dressed only in the thinnest of rags, torn and patched, and that their thin bodies showed through the holes and tatters in a manner piteous to see. Now and again they shivered, but not for a moment did they stop working until all the shoes were finished and ready. Then they tidied up the needles and thread, placed the shoes neatly in pairs along the bench, and vanished as silently as they had come. When Gregory and Joan came out of hiding, their secret helpers were nowhere to be seen.

'Those poor little elves,' said Joan. 'Did you see how miserably they were clothed?'

'Did you see how cold they were this frosty night?' said Gregory, who was a little cold himself, in spite of his warm clothes.

'I tell you what, Husband,' said Joan. 'Instead of giving them work tonight, let us make them some clothes. We have plenty of shoes in stock, thanks to them.'

'Yes, indeed,' agreed Gregory. 'We scarcely need their help any more. My work is so highly prized that I have all the trade I want and more. Besides, I am strong and well and can easily look after our needs without help. This big stock of leather will last us through the winter, and perhaps we could even afford to take a little holiday.'

So it was agreed. Joan spent all day making two little shirts of warm flannel, two pairs of trousers, two pairs of woollen stockings and two little caps to protect the elves' heads. Gregory made two neat pairs of shoes out of soft red leather. At night they left some supper for the elves and a bit of fire in the grate. Then they went to bed, for they were very tired after their day's work. They had had little sleep the night before.

When morning came, Gregory and Joan went downstairs to see what had become of their presents. The fire was out, the food was eaten, and there was no sign of the little clothes they had made the day before.

The shoemaker and his wife never saw their secret helpers again, and the little men did not come, for there was no need of them. What had happened in the night was this.

As soon as the elves arrived in the workshop, promptly at midnight, they had skipped on to the bench to begin

work. But they were surprised and delighted to find the two suits of clothes and the two pairs of shoes laid out for them. Immediately they danced with joy, threw their old rags into the fire and put on the new clothes. Then they sat down to supper on the hearth and finished every scrap the good shoemaker's wife had left them.

'Now,' cried one elf to the other, 'we have fine suits of warm clothes. We can live like gentlemen at last, and need do no more shoemaking.'

So away they skipped, vanishing as they had come, and not a sign did they leave except two empty bowls, each with a spoon in it.

The Woodcutter's Third Son

'FATHER,' said the woodcutter's eldest son one day, 'I am old enough to go into the forest by myself and cut wood. Lend me an axe and let me go.'

The woodcutter's eldest son was a clever boy, tall and handsome, and everyone praised him.

'Very well,' said his father. 'Here is an axe. But mind, it is sharp, so be careful.'

His wife gave the boy a basket containing a bottle of sweet wine and a rich cake. The eldest son went striding off into the forest with his axe over his shoulder and his basket in one hand.

When he came to the forest, he met a little old man with almost no hair on the top of his head and a long grey beard on his chin.

'My name is Grizkin,' said the old man, 'and I have a great hunger and thirst. Let me taste of your food and drink.'

'Certainly not,' said the eldest son. 'If I give you cake and wine, I shall have less for myself. Be off with you, old man.'

'You will be sorry for this, young master,' said Grizkin, and shuffled away among the trees.

The eldest son sat down to eat his cake and drink his wine. Then he placed himself at the foot of a tree and raised his axe.

But at the very first stroke, he cut his arm and cried out in pain. Without making another stroke, he picked up his axe and went home. That was the end of *his* woodcutting.

'Father,' said the second son, 'let *me* go into the forest and cut wood.'

'Very well,' said his father, 'you are a clever fellow, and perhaps you will fare better than your brother.'

So the second son was given a sharp axe and a basket containing a bottle of wine and a cake. Off he went into the forest with the axe over his shoulder and the basket in his hand.

When he got to the forest, out came Grizkin.

'I have a terrible hunger and thirst,' said the old man. 'Please give me something to eat and drink from your basket.'

'Not a crumb,' said the clever boy, 'not a sip do you get! If I shared my wine and cake with you, there might not be enough for me! Be off with you, old man, and go begging somewhere else.'

'You will be sorry for this, young master,' said Grizkin, and once more shuffled away among the trees.

Well, the second son, clever though he was, fared no better than his brother. At the very first stroke of his axe, he missed the tree he was aiming at and struck himself in the ankle. Howling with pain, he picked up the axe and the basket and limped off home.

'Father,' said the woodcutter's third son, 'let me go into the forest and cut wood. I have watched you do it, and I know how. I am quite old enough to cut wood by myself.'

At this they all laughed. For the third son, who was a short, plain boy, was known as Little Woodenhead because everyone thought him stupid.

When they had finished laughing at Woodenhead, his father said, 'Well, I suppose you may learn some sense if you too hurt yourself. Here is an axe. Be off with you, and see if you can manage not to kill yourself outright.'

'Thank you, father,' said Woodenhead. 'Give me some wine and cake too, mother, in case I get hungry.'

'There is no wine and cake for a stupid boy like you,' said his mother. 'All I can give you is this bottle of water and this loaf of stale bread.'

'That will do,' said Woodenhead cheerfully, and taking up the axe and the basket, ran off to the forest.

When he got there, out stepped old Grizkin from behind a tree.

'I am hungry and thirsty, young man,' he said. 'Give me some of your wine and cake.'

'I have no wine and cake,' said Woodenhead politely, 'but if you like to share my bread and water, you are welcome.'

So the two of them sat down together and finished the stale loaf and the water between them.

'I don't think much of that,' said Grizkin, 'but it's better than nothing. I shan't forget your kindness, young fellow. You shall have good luck this day.'

So saying he shook the crumbs from his beard and shuffled off among the trees, and Woodenhead picked up his axe and began to look for a likely tree.

Now any sensible young man would have chosen a small tree on which to begin his work as a woodcutter. But Woodenhead, being foolish, chose the largest tree in the forest. It was a great hollow oak. Woodenhead hacked and hewed with a will, and at last the tree, being hollow, fell with a crash. There inside it, sitting on the ground, was a goose covered all over with golden feathers.

'H'm,' said Woodenhead, 'that's not such a bad bird. I suppose that's what the old man meant by good luck.'

So he picked up the golden goose, tucked it under his arm, and made off.

By the time he got out of the forest, it was late, and he made up his mind to spend the night at an inn.

Now the landlord of the inn had three daughters. They were not in the least interested in the plain little Woodenhead, but they were very interested in the goose.

As soon as Woodenhead was out of the way the eldest thought she would like one of the golden feathers. But no sooner had she grasped the bird's tail than her hand stuck fast, and she could not get it away.

Then in came the landlord's second daughter. She too thought she would like a golden feather. But before her sister could warn her, she had touched the goose, and she too was held fast. Tug as she would, she could not get herself free.

Then along came the third daughter, and the same thing happened to her. So all three sisters had to spend the night stuck fast to the golden goose.

In the morning little Woodenhead got up early and decided to go home. So, taking no notice of the three girls, he picked up the goose, tucked it under his arm and set off at a good pace. All that the three sisters could do was to trot along behind Woodenhead, going just where he took them, because their hands were stuck fast to the goose.

When they were crossing a field, the parson of the village saw them and called out, 'Hey there! Why are you three girls running after this young fellow? That is no way to go on. Leave him alone, I say!'

He ran after Woodenhead and the three girls, and no sooner had he grasped the youngest of the sisters by the

hand than he too stuck fast, and was obliged to trot along behind.

Before long the sexton came that way and was astonished to see the parson running after Woodenhead and the three girls, puffing and blowing and holding his hat on his head with one hand.

'Oh sir,' cried the sexton, 'whatever are you doing running after this fellow with the goose and the three girls? Come back, sir, I beg. Don't you remember we have a wedding to perform today?'

So saying he grabbed the parson by the arm. But he too stuck fast and could only run along at the tail of the procession.

Soon two farm labourers came in sight and the sexton called out to them to set him and the parson free. Dropping their tools, the two men got hold of the sexton. But it was no use. Pull as they might, they too stuck fast to the sexton, so now there were seven of them running along behind Woodenhead and the goose – the three girls, the parson, the sexton, and the two labourers.

Well, off they trotted at a smart pace, for Woodenhead only wanted to get home with the golden goose he had found inside the hollow tree. But by this time he had lost the way, and presently he found himself in a strange city. Here ruled a King with one daughter, a beautiful and very serious Princess. So serious was the Princess that nothing could make her laugh.

The King and the Queen were so worried about her seriousness that they thought she must be unhappy and would soon pine away altogether. They offered her hand in marriage to anyone who could make their daughter laugh. So rich was the King, and so beautiful his daughter, that great Princes and Dukes came from far and near to make her laugh and gain her hand in marriage. But nothing they did could raise so much as the ghost of a smile on the Princess's pale, beautiful face. They were funny enough, some of them, and other people laughed – but not the Princess.

Now, on the day that Woodenhead with his goose and his seven followers came into the city, it chanced that the Princess was sitting at her window, looking more solemn than ever. When she heard the noise of the strange procession, she got up from her chair and looked down into the street. There was plain Woodenhead and his goose, the three sisters, the parson, the sexton and the labourers all jostling each other and trying to pull themselves away, puffing and blowing and calling for help.

So comic was the sight, and so unlike anything else she had ever seen, that the Princess's face broke into a smile. Then her smile grew broader, and at last she gave a great peal of merriment, and didn't stop laughing for a full half-hour by the great city clock in the tower on the Guildhall.

Now Woodenhead, as you know, was a plain little

fellow, but the Princess took a fancy to him. The King and Queen were not too pleased at the thought of having a woodcutter's plain son for their son-in-law, but the Princess would not hear of giving him up. So they were married amid pomp and rejoicing. They lived to be a great age, and the Princess never grew tired of her husband, for he could always make her laugh when she was feeling downcast.

The King's Servant

'THE Queen's ring has been stolen. Who has taken it? Stephen, the King's servant – he is the thief!'

So they were saying in the palace. The Queen had lost her ring. Everyone said it was Stephen who had taken it.

But Stephen had not taken the ring. Something quite different had happened that day. His master, the King, was the wisest man in the world. It seemed as if he knew everything – the secrets of the sky and the sea, the secrets of the weather and the seasons, the secrets of men and beasts. The wise King knew them all. This was how he knew them. Every day, after dinner, he stayed in the dining-hall alone, and Stephen, his faithful servant, brought him a little covered dish. Then he retired. Soon afterwards the King sent for Stephen, who took the dish away.

Now on the day when the Queen lost her ring, Stephen had been overcome by curiosity and had looked into the King's dish after the King had sent for him to take it away. Under the cover he had found a little white snake. This was the serpent of wisdom, though Stephen did not know it. He could not resist finding out how it tasted. So he cut off a little piece and put it in his mouth. Then he covered the dish once more and took it back to the pantry.

Looking out of the window, he at once heard a chattering among the birds and a whispering in the leaves. All were telling each other the secrets of the court, the secrets of the weather and the seasons, the secrets of the wind and the waves. So this was how the King had learned everything he knew!

But what use was it to Stephen to have the secret of all wisdom? He was accused of stealing the Queen's ring. If he did not find it that very day, he was to be put to death in the morning. Anxious and fearful for his life, he walked out and stood by a duck-pond behind the castle. At once he heard three ducks talking and gossiping together.

'I found a fine fat worm this morning,' said one of them.

'And I had a little frog,' said another. 'How delicious it tasted.'

'As for me,' said the third duck, 'I have eaten I know not what. It was round and bright. I found it at the bottom of the pond. I gobbled it up, and it has given me a stomach-ache. I shall die because of my greed.'

At once Stephen guessed what had happened. Seizing the duck, he ran with it to the kitchen, and asked the cook to kill and dress it for supper. The cook did so, and inside it was found the Queen's ring.

The King was so sorry that Stephen had been wrongly

accused that he told him he could have anything he wanted.

'All I want, Sire,' said the trusty servant, 'is a horse and my freedom for a while, that I may go and explore the wide world.'

The King gave him what he wanted, and next morning Stephen rode away from the castle upon a fine grey horse that his master had given him.

Away went Stephen into the wide world. One day he

saw three fishes gasping for breath in the reeds at the edge of a lake.

'Alas,' they sighed, 'if we can't get back into the water, we shall die.'

Of course Stephen could understand what they said, for he had the secret of wisdom. At once he jumped off his horse and put the three fishes carefully back into the lake.

'Oh thank you,' they cried. 'We shall never forget your kindness. One day we will reward you.'

Once more Stephen mounted the grey horse and trotted off into the wide world. He came to a forest with a winding path leading through the trees.

Suddenly he heard a tiny voice complaining. It was the King of the Ants.

'What a clumsy brute that horse is!' wailed the Ant King. 'Look at him, trampling down my people with his great hooves.'

At once Stephen was sorry at what he heard and turned his horse aside so as not to trample upon the ants.

'Oh thank you, young man!' cried the Ant King. 'We shall not forget your kindness to tiny helpless creatures. One day we will reward you.'

Stephen rode on, and at the end of the forest he saw two baby crows who had tumbled out of their nest while their parents were away looking for food.

'Alas,' they said miserably, 'we can't fly, and here on the ground we shall be killed or starve for want of food.'

At once Stephen got off his horse, picked up the two little crows, climbed the tree and put them safely back in the nest.

The young man continued on his way, and at last he came to a great city. Here lived a King who had a beautiful daughter. A herald went about the streets crying out that the King would give her in marriage to any young man who could perform a hard and dangerous task. If he failed, his head would be cut off. Most of the young men in the city were too frightened to offer themselves as suitors, but, as soon as he saw the beauty of the Princess, Stephen was determined to try.

Stephen presented himself to the King and said he was ready to perform the task. At once he was led to the sea-shore, and a precious stone was thrown over a cliff into the water. He was told that he must fetch it back and return it to the King. Everyone was sad, for Stephen was a handsome young man, and it seemed a pity that he should die. For how could anyone be expected to get back a jewel thrown from a cliff into the deep sea?

Stephen went down to the edge of the water and considered what he should do. Then he saw swimming towards him the very same three fishes whose lives he had saved. One of them carried in its mouth the jewel, and this he laid at the young man's feet.

'Here is your reward for saving our lives,' said the

fish, and with a flick of its tail it swam away into the deep sea, followed by its two companions.

Stephen picked up the precious stone and ran with it in haste to the palace.

But the beautiful Princess was proud of heart. Although Stephen had performed the task he had been set, she knew that he was only a servant.

'Before I marry him,' she said, 'he must perform another task.'

So she led Stephen to a garden and ordered ten sacks full of fine seed to be brought. With her own hand she emptied the seeds on to the grass and told Stephen that he must put them all back into the sacks and leave not one grain behind.

Now there were hundreds and thousands of seeds, and Stephen had not the least idea how he could put them all back into the sacks. So he went sadly to sleep under a tree and awaited the morning, when he knew he must die.

But when morning came, all the seeds were back in their sacks exactly as they had been before the Princess had scattered them on the grass. It was the King of the Ants who, with his great army of followers, had come in the night and put the seeds back. Had he not promised that Stephen should be rewarded for his kindness to the ant people?

The Princess was not sure she was pleased that Stephen had performed the second task. She liked the look of him, but her proud heart could not bear the thought of marriage to a serving man.

'I cannot marry you,' she said, 'until you do one more thing. Go and fetch me an apple from the tree of life, and after I have eaten it, I will be your bride.'

Once more Stephen set off. His heart was heavy, for he had no idea where to find the tree of life. He thought he would wander off into the wide world and never set eyes upon the Princess again.

Through three kingdoms he wandered, looking for the tree of life, until from sheer weariness he sank down at the edge of a wood. Just then he heard something stirring in the leaves above him. All at once a golden apple fell on the ground beside him, and the two crows fluttered down, and alighted one on each of his shoulders.

'We are the birds whose lives you saved,' they said. 'We have repaid you for your kindness. Take the apple and marry your Princess.'

With a whirl of black feathers they were off. Gladly Stephen picked up the apple and started back towards the city where the Princess lived.

The Princess had begun to miss the poor young man whom she had sent off into the world, so she was full of gladness to see him return at last. He gave her the apple, and together they sat down and ate it. All at once her heart overflowed with love for him. Soon they were married, and they lived as happily as any couple since the beginning of time.

The Cock, the Cat and the Scythe

OLD Matthew was a countryman living with his three sons in a cottage at the edge of a farm. He was very ancient and infirm. His eyes were dim, his voice weak, and his legs so feeble that before long he took to his bed. He had had a good life, though he had never saved any money. He was content to die, and only wished he had something to leave to his three sons, Peter, John and Colin.

When he knew that his time had come, he called the three boys to his bedside and said in a quavering voice,

'I must soon leave you, my sons, and I am sorry I have not much to give you. But what I have is yours. Peter, you shall have this fine cock with his tall red comb and his feathers of green and gold.'

Peter took the cock and thanked his father. It was indeed a fine bird.

'You, John,' went on the old man, 'shall have my cat. He is not much to look at, but he is a good mouser. No place where he stays shall ever be troubled with mice.'

John thanked the old man and took the cat. Then Matthew went on in his feeble voice, 'As for you, Colin, I have nothing to give you but my scythe. With it I have cut corn and mowed grass for many years. It is a good scythe. Take it, and may you have good luck. These things are not much, but take them to lands where they are not known, and you shall learn their true value.'

Then Matthew closed his eyes and fell asleep.

After the old man's death Peter took the cock and set out. But everywhere he went, he found that people had plenty of cocks and would give him nothing for such a common bird. In the towns he saw that the church spires had gold cocks upon them to tell which way the wind was blowing, and in the country every farmyard had at least one cock to wake the people every morning.

But Peter never gave up hope, and one day he reached an island where there were no cocks, and where no such bird had ever been seen. He showed the people the bird and said, 'Look at him! See his tall red comb and his feathers of green and gold.'

'He is indeed splendid to look at,' said the people, 'but of what use is he?'

'He will wake you every morning at the same time,' said Peter. 'As it is, you never know when to get up. Some of you sleep so long that you waste the best part of the day. Besides, every night, at regular intervals, he crows three times. But if he crows during daylight, you shall know that there is to be a change in the weather. Believe me, there never was a more useful bird in the world.'

'You are right,' said the people, 'but is he for sale? How much do you want for him?'

'I must have a donkey laden with as much gold as it can carry.'

'Done!' said the people, who had plenty of gold. 'That is not much to pay for such a fine bird.'

So they gave Peter what he asked for, and off he went with his donkey laden with gold. Two great baskets it carried, and when Peter got home, his brothers were delighted.

'I too will go and make my fortune,' said John.

So off he went with the cat.

But everywhere he went the people had all the cats they needed – black cats, white cats, ginger cats and tabbies. They only laughed at John and told him to take his cat away and find something more useful. So off he went, till at last he came to an island where there were no cats. As you can imagine, the houses were overrun with mice. The people had done all they could to get rid of them, but still they came in their hundreds and ate up the corn and the cheese and the bread in their homes. No sooner had John let his cat loose than it caught a mouse, and then another and another and another, till everyone saw what a useful creature it was.

'That's not such a bad animal,' they said. 'It's not much

to look at, but we can do with an animal like that. How much do you want for him?'

'I will let you have him,' said John, 'for as much gold as a horse can carry on its back.' They agreed that this was not much to pay for the cat, so they gladly gave John what he asked for. When John at last got home with his horse laden with gold, his brothers were overjoyed. It was now the turn of Colin to see what luck he would have. So one bright morning, he sharpened the scythe his father had left him, and set off into the world.

But everywhere he went, he found that the men carried scythes over their shoulders and went out each morning to cut the hay and the corn.

'Won't you buy my scythe?' he asked. 'It is a good scythe and used to belong to my father.'

'We can see that,' said the men, 'for it is a very old-fashioned scythe. We have better ones ourselves. Be off with you and see if you can find somebody who has never seen a scythe.'

Well, this was exactly what Colin did. One day he reached an island where no scythe had ever been seen. Yet the fields were full of ripe corn, and Colin waited to see how the people would harvest it. When the time came, he was amazed to see that they did not cut the corn down, but shot it down with cannons! All the guns on the island were brought out and fired off with tremendous noise and smoke. The farm animals were terrified;

dogs barked, cats howled, and hens and geese were too frightened to lay. Nor was this a very good way of harvesting the corn, for some of it was shot near the top and the grain destroyed; some of the cannons fired right over the fields, and some of the cannon-balls were so hot that they set fire to the corn and burned it to the ground.

This was Colin's chance. He shouldered his scythe, and without noise or fuss cut down all the corn in one field before the people could get at it with the cannons. They were so pleased that they asked him how much he would take for his scythe.

'That's much better than guns,' they said. 'Such an invention is worth having.'

Colin told them they could have his scythe for a handcart full of gold, and this they gladly gave him. So off he went without his scythe but with a handcart of gold, which he pushed before him. When his brothers saw him, they were full of gladness. They prepared a noble feast to celebrate his home-coming, and afterwards they put all their money together and bought a big farm on which they worked in peace and friendship for many years. You can be sure of one thing – or rather, of three things. They bought themselves first a cock, to wake them in the morning, and next a cat, to keep down the mice in their barns. When harvest-time came round, they and their men worked with scythes to cut the corn, and never, never tried shooting it down with cannons.

The Biggest Turnip in the World

A CART was being driven along the road. The driver was a young man named Barney. In the cart was the strangest thing ever seen, and people crowded the roadside to have a look at it. It was round and white, and one end was pointed, and on the other grew a bunch of green leaves. It was shaped exactly like a turnip, but it was much, much bigger than any turnip that ever grew before. Yes, that is what it was – the biggest turnip in the world. It took two oxen to draw it.

'That is surely not a turnip,' said one passer-by.

'It must be a turnip,' said another, 'but it is a very big turnip.'

'It is not only big,' said a third. 'It is enormous. Why, it must be the most enormous turnip in the world.'

Barney took no notice of what they said, but went on driving the two oxen and the cart with the turnip in it. This is how it was. Barney was the younger of two brothers. His elder brother, Francis, was very rich, but Barney had nothing but one field and a cottage. Francis had meadows and herds, horses and money. But he was mean. He gave his poor brother nothing.

That spring Barney had planted his whole field with turnip seed. Soon he had a fine crop of young turnips, but one in particular grew better than the rest. It grew and grew, until it was the biggest turnip in the world.

'But what use is it?' said Barney to himself. 'If I eat it, I shall waste all the other turnips, for this one would last me the whole winter. I can't sell it, for who would want to buy such a monstrous vegetable? If I leave it to rot, it will make a dreadful mess and smell bad. I can't leave it to grow for ever, for it might take up my whole field. No, there is only one thing to do with such a turnip. I will give it to the King. That is what people do with such things.'

So he borrowed a cart and two oxen from a neighbour, and the neighbour and his men helped Barney load the turnip on to the cart. Off he went along the highroad to the King's palace.

When he reached the palace, he was shown into the presence of the King, who came out to see what he had brought.

'Your Majesty,' said Barney, bowing low, 'this wonder has grown in my field, and I would like to present it to you. It is said to be the biggest turnip in the world.'

'Indeed I am sure it is,' said the King.

He was touched by Barney's wish to present such a marvel to him, and he knew that everyone who came to his court would be amazed to see such an extraordinary thing.

'That is most kind of you,' he told Barney, 'and I will be glad to accept your gift. You must indeed be a fortunate young man to be blessed with such a marvel.'

'No indeed, Your Majesty,' said Barney. 'I am a poor unfortunate young man. I have very little in the world, while my elder brother has horses and cattle, money and land.'

'If that is so,' answered the King, 'I shall make you

as rich as your brother. Such ill-fortune deserves to be rewarded.'

The King was as good as his word. He gave Barney a big patch of rich land, a herd of cows, two fine horses and much money.

Well, when Barney's brother Francis heard what had happened to Barney, he grew very envious, rich as he was.

'I too will take a present to the King,' he said. 'But

I will give him something better than a turnip. I will take his Majesty my finest horse, a pair of oxen, and several choice jewels.'

He rode in his coach with the jewels, and a stable-man followed behind with the animals. When he got to the palace he was shown into the royal presence.

He offered his gifts to the King, who graciously accepted them.

'You are indeed a fortunate man,' said the King. 'But how can I reward one who seems to be almost as rich as I am, and to have everything he needs? You have cattle and land, money and fine clothes. I daresay you have a splendid house as well. Now what shall I give you?'

The King stroked his beard thoughtfully.

'I tell you what,' he said at last. 'I have one thing which I doubt if you can equal. A young man brought it to me the other day. It is the biggest turnip in the world. Of course I prize it highly as a wonder and a marvel, but I will present it to you as your reward for bringing me gifts.'

So Francis was forced to take the enormous turnip, since it would not do to refuse a gift from the King. Back home he went, with the turnip tied to the top of his coach. What he did with it when he got back home I really don't know.

The Enchanted Wood

LISBETH sat miserably under a tree in the middle of a wood and cried bitterly.

'Whatever shall I do?' she sobbed. 'I am quite alone. I shall never get out of this wood. There is nothing to eat, and if I am not killed by wild animals, I shall starve to death.'

She did not know that the place where she was lost was an enchanted wood. She was a poor servant-girl, and she had been travelling in a coach with her master and mistress. The party had been attacked by robbers, who had killed the coachman and stolen everything of value in the coach. The master and mistress had been chased far into the wood by the robbers, and what became of them Lisbeth never found out. As for herself, she had escaped by hiding in a dense thicket.

It was useless to wander farther. She was lost. So she sat on the ground at the foot of a tree, waiting to see what would happen.

She had almost fallen asleep through weariness when she heard the sound of wings, and a white pigeon fluttered to the ground at her side. It placed in her open hand a little gold key it had been carrying in its beak. Then it spoke.

'In that big tree over there,' the pigeon said, 'is a little door. Open it with the key and go inside.'

Somehow Lisbeth, though surprised to hear the bird speak, had no fear, and at once did as it had said. She took the key to the great tree, and there, sure enough, was a little door just wide enough for her to enter. She unlocked it, and found herself in a room, small but bright and airy. On a table was milk and bread, so that she was

able to satisfy hunger and thirst. Against a wall was a white bed, soft, dry and comfortable.

The pigeon alighted at the door and said, 'Make use of this room as if it were your own. I will visit you each day and give you all you need. Don't be afraid. Sleep well.'

Then it flew off, and Lisbeth was left alone. She was so tired that she lay down on the bed and fell asleep instantly. In the morning she discovered that there was a clothes cupboard in one wall. She opened it and found it full of rich dresses set with costly ornaments. It seemed that these too were meant for her.

So she lived in content and safety in the enchanted wood, and every evening the pigeon came and talked to her and asked if there was anything she wanted.

One day the pigeon said to Lisbeth, 'Will you do something for me now?'

Lisbeth said she would be glad to, and the bird went on, 'Take that path there until it brings you to a little house. Go in, and you will see an old woman sitting by the fire. She will bid you good-day, but whatever you do, take no notice of her. Pass by her, and at the farther end of the room you will see a door. Go through it, and on a table you will see many rings set with jewels and precious stones. Leave these alone, but find a plain ring which is kept among the others. Bring this to me, for I need it, but on no account speak to the woman.'

Lisbeth did exactly as the bird told her. She found the little house and entered it.

The old woman by the fire said, 'Good day to you, girl. What can I do for you?'

But Lisbeth took no notice, and went on into the farther room. There was the table, laden with fine rings of silver and gold inset with gleaming stones. She looked for a plain ring, but could find none. Then she glanced back through the door and saw that the old woman was stealing away with a bird-cage in her hand.

Lisbeth stepped up to the old woman and took the cage from her. Inside it was a bird, and the bird held in its beak a ring of plain silver.

'What are you doing?' the old woman said shrilly. 'Give me back the cage! It's mine.'

But the girl took no notice and slipped her finger and thumb between the bars of the cage. She took the ring from the bird's beak and ran back into the wood by the way she had come.

When she got back to the room in the tree where she lived, she expected that the white pigeon would come and take the ring it had asked for. But the pigeon did not appear, so Lisbeth walked a little farther, calling to the bird to come. Still there was no pigeon. So she leaned against a tall tree and waited. As she leaned against its trunk, suddenly it began to grow soft, and two of its branches slowly bent down towards her. They had turned into arms. Strange as this was, Lisbeth was not afraid, for she had learned to have no fear in the enchanted wood.

The two arms twined about the girl. When she looked up, she saw that the tree was no longer a tree but a young man, tall and handsome, who kissed her and embraced her very lovingly.

'I thank you, Lisbeth,' said the young man softly, 'for delivering me from the power of the old woman. She is a wicked witch. Once when I was going through the forest with my servants, she bewitched me and turned me into a tree. Each evening I became for a short time a white pigeon. This is how I was able to help you when you were lost in the wood. So long as she kept my plain silver ring, she had power over me, and I could not get back to my human shape. I was afraid that I should spend the whole of my life as a tree or a pigeon, but your kindness and courage have overcome the power of the witch. I am a prince. I love you, and if you will have me, I will make you my princess.'

Then Lisbeth marvelled at what had happened, and she was even more surprised when the other trees which had stood around the prince turned into his servants and horses. It was a joyful sight to see all of them freed from the enchantments of the wicked witch. Together they rode out of the wood, and set off in search of the prince's kingdom. There he married Lisbeth and lived with her in freedom and happiness.

The Travelling Band

HAVE you ever heard of a band of travelling animals? No, not a circus – a real travelling band. Well, the story starts with an old donkey who was afraid his master would get rid of him. One day he overheard the farmer say to himself, 'I'll have to get rid of that donkey. He's too old and feeble to pull a cart any more, and he's not worth the food he eats.'

The donkey thought this cruel, for had he not worked faithfully for many years, and what did it cost his master to let him eat thistles at the end of the yard?

'I know what I'll do,' said the donkey to himself. 'I'll start a travelling band. I can still make a fine noise, just like some of those trumpeters I've heard when the soldiers are passing. That's what I'll do.'

So one fine morning he kicked up his heels as best he could and went off down the lane at a comfortable trot. He hadn't been on the road long before he met an old hound.

'Good morning,' said the donkey. 'You look pretty miserable. What's the matter?'

The old hound snuffled and wheezed, and then he said, 'I'm not long for this world. My master is a huntsman,

and I heard him tell the stableman he'd have to get rid of me. Says I'm too slow for hunting and not worth the meat I eat – though goodness knows that's little enough.'

The poor dog's face and ears hung down as if he was going to cry, and his tail drooped between his legs as if he had never wagged it in his life.

'Can you bark?' asked the donkey. 'Give us a taste of your voice.'

The hound lifted up his head, opened his mouth and uttered a long mournful cry.

'Why, that's splendid!' said the donkey. 'You're just the fellow I need. Come along and join my band. People will travel miles to hear musicians like us. What with my bray and your bark, we'll be earning our living in no time.'

So the hound joined the donkey and together they

trotted along the road. Very soon they met an old tabby cat with a face like three rainy days.

'What's wrong with you?' asked the donkey.

The cat gave a melancholy miaou and said, 'My mistress has driven me out. She says I'm getting blind and my teeth have fallen out, so I'm no use for mousing any more. I'm not worth the milk I drink – that's what she says. But goodness knows it's little enough she gives me.'

'You can still give a fine catcall, I dare say,' said the donkey. 'Let's hear you.'

So the poor old cat lifted up her head, opened her toothless jaws and wailed as loud as she could.

'Why, that's fine. You're just the girl we're looking for. Come and join our band. What with my bray, the dog's bark and your operatic skill, we'll be as fine a band as any in the world.'

So off they went together. Before long they met a cock with a very doleful countenance. His tail feathers dragged along the ground and his comb was pale and drooping.

'What's wrong with you?' inquired the donkey. 'What are you doing all by yourself on the roads?'

'I've run away,' said the cock. 'Only thing to do. Master's got visitors coming on Sunday, and I heard him tell the cook to get me ready for the stewpot. How would you like that?'

'I've never heard of stewed donkey,' answered the

donkey. 'But I've troubles of my own. Now you're just the fellow we want. I needn't ask if you're a musician, for everyone knows you are. How would you like to join our travelling band?'

The cock readily agreed, and crowed with pleasure. At this the cat began howling, the dog barked, and the donkey joined in with a loud 'Hee-haw!'

When they had all finished, the donkey said, 'That's not half bad for a first try. We'll soon be earning our living at that rate.'

So off they went, all four of them, and as darkness came on, they found themselves in a forest. Here they prepared to spend the night. The donkey lay on the ground beneath a tree; the old hound curled up beside him; the cat climbed on to a branch, and the cock flew to the top of the tree. He looked round and soon made out with his keen eyes a glimmer of light from a cottage not far off.

'I think we'd be more comfortable over there,' he said. 'It's getting cold out here, and besides, we might find a bite to eat.'

Now the cottage belonged to a robber band, who, just at that moment, were sitting down to supper after a hard day's burglary. The donkey looked in at the window and saw them as they sat round a table in a room where a warm fire was burning.

'Let's give them some music,' said the donkey. 'Then

perhaps they'll let us come in and give us something to eat.'

So the donkey stood under the window, the hound got up on his back, the cat climbed on to the hound and the cock perched himself on top of the cat.

'Now then,' said the donkey. 'Let's surprise them. One! two! three! four!'

Then immediately they all made as much noise as they

could. The donkey brayed, the hound barked, the cat miaoued and the cock crowed as if it was the day of judgement. At this terrible sound the robbers dropped their knives, jumped up from the table and rushed out of doors into the woods. They thought they had been surprised by demons or witches, so they went and hid in the bushes as fast as their legs would take them. At this moment the donkey broke the window, and all the animals jumped into the warm room and fell to with a will on the food laid out on the table. They ate everything they could find, for they were all hungry and none had eaten a square meal since leaving home. When they had had enough, they blew out the lights and settled down for the night. The cat stretched herself on the hearth; the hound lay by the door; the cock perched on a beam overhead, while the donkey went out into the yard.

At last, when all was quiet and the fire had died down so that the cottage was in darkness, the robbers crept back, and the bravest of them tiptoed inside. Seeing the two bright eyes of the cat on the hearth, he mistook them for the last sparks of the fire. So he took a taper from his pocket and held it towards the cat, to get a light for the candles. At once the cat screamed at the robber and spat at him fiercely. The robber, taken by surprise, ran from the cottage, and as he did so, the dog bit him in the ankle and the cock screamed 'Cock-a-doodle-do!' Then the donkey in the yard gave him a kick as he passed, so that by the time the robber got back to his companions, he was trembling with terror and hardly able to speak.

'The p-p-place is haunted,' he told his companions, as soon as he could make himself understood. 'There was an old w-w-witch by the fire who spat at me. A man was standing by the d-door and cut me in the leg with a knife. When I got outside, there was a black m-monster who hit me with a wooden club. And there was a demon who had turned himself into a cock and was shouting 'Cut the devil in two!' I'm not going back into that house, not if you give me all the gold we've ever taken.'

Well, none of the robbers dared go back into the cottage, so the animals' travelling band took possession of it. There they settled down to live peacefully together. They practised their music, and nobody troubled them, as the cottage was believed to be haunted. When they ran short of food, off they went together and performed at fairs and markets. Soon they became famous and were never again without a roof over their heads and money to buy food with.

Three Simpletons

'I AM off to town,' said Thomas the farmer, taking up his thick ash stick, 'and I shan't be home till Monday. I've been expecting the cattle dealer, who promised to come and have a look at those three cows in the byre. But he hasn't turned up, and I can't wait any longer.'

'Very well, dear,' said his wife Martha. 'What shall I do if he comes while you're away?'

'You can let him have the cows,' said Thomas, 'but mind – don't take a penny less than fifty pounds. You're such a stupid woman that I half expect you to make a mess of the bargain. But there's no help for it. Now mind – at least fifty pounds, do you hear?'

'I'll remember, Tom,' said Martha.

Thomas was not really a bad-tempered man, but his wife was a real simpleton, and her stupidity had often given him trouble.

'Now if you do anything foolish,' Thomas said, grasping his stick and going out of the door, 'I'll give you a beating you'll never forget.'

Martha smiled, waved good-bye, and turned to get on with her work.

Next day the dealer came to make an offer for the cows.

'My husband's away,' said Martha, 'but you can take the cows for a fair price.'

'I'll give you forty pounds,' said the dealer. 'They're hardly worth it, but that's what I'll give you.'

Martha remembered what her husband had said.

'No,' she said, 'not a penny less than fifty pounds.'

'You drive a hard bargain,' said the dealer. 'But I'll give you what you ask.'

So he unfastened the cows and began leading them out of the yard.

'Here,' said Martha, determined not to be foolish. 'You haven't paid me. Where's the fifty pounds?'

'Bless my soul,' said the dealer, 'if I haven't forgotten my purse! I'll tell you what,' he added cunningly, 'I'll take two of the three cows, and leave you the other as a pledge until I come next time with the money.'

'That seems fair,' said poor Martha, not knowing how she was being cheated. 'Take the two, and don't forget the money when you come for the third one.'

'I won't,' said the dealer, as he led the two cows out of the yard.

'Not a penny less than fifty pounds!' called Martha after him.

When her husband returned, she told him what had happened.

'I've sold the three cows,' she said. 'I got fifty pounds for them, as you said.'

'Where's the money?' asked Thomas.

Martha told him how the dealer had promised to bring the money when he came for the third cow.

'I let him take the two fattest,' she said, 'so that we've only the lean one to feed till he comes back.'

'Why you simpleton!' roared the farmer. 'He'll never come back – not now he's got my two best cows for nothing. You really are the stupidest woman I ever knew!'

He raised his stick to beat her with, but then thought better of it.

'I'm going out on to the highway,' he said, 'to see if there's a stupider woman in the world. If there is, I'll never beat you again. I just want to find out how stupid people can be.'

So off he went, and presently he heard the sound of a horse and cart. Round the corner came old Margery, standing up in her cart and holding the reins in her hand. Beside her in the cart was a bundle of straw.

'Now why on earth doesn't she sit on the straw and rest herself?' said Thomas. 'She must be as stupid as my wife. Let's see how simple she is.'

So he jumped up and down in front of the cart, and the woman drew rein and stopped the horse.

'What do you want, stranger?' asked Margery. 'Who are you, and where do you come from?'

'I come straight from Heaven,' answered Thomas, to see if the woman would believe him. 'I've just fallen down and I can't get back. Do you think you could drive me there?'

'Why no,' said Margery, 'for I don't know the way. But if you come from Heaven, perhaps you know my husband, who has been there these two years.'

'What's he like?' asked Thomas.

'He's a short, bald man,' Margery answered, 'and his name is Harry.'

'I know him well,' said Thomas. 'He's in trouble, though. His job is to drive sheep about on the hillside, and they're always going astray. His clothes are in rags and he has nothing to buy new ones with.'

'Oh dear,' said Margery, 'my poor Harry. If only you could do something for him. I tell you what: I have just been to market and sold my corn for forty pounds. Do you think you could take it to my husband in Heaven?'

'Why, certainly,' said Thomas.

So she gave him a leather bag containing forty pounds, and said, 'That's very kind of you, sir! I know my poor Harry will be glad of the money. My son and I are quite well off, and we can easily do without it.'

'Before you go,' said Thomas, 'tell me one thing. Why do you stand up in your cart instead of sitting on that bundle of straw and resting yourself?'

'Oh, I always travel like this,' answered Margery. 'It makes the load easier for my old horse!'

Off she went, and the farmer was left in amazement at finding anyone so foolish as Margery.

'Why, this woman is even stupider than my wife,' he said to himself.

Then he walked on till he came to an ale-house, where he sat down on a bench outside, to refresh himself.

As soon as Margery got home, she told her son what had happened.

'Wasn't I lucky,' she said, 'to find a man who is going to Heaven and can take our money to your poor father?'

'Why yes,' said her son. 'But my father is old, and perhaps he has need of a horse. If I could catch up the man, perhaps he could take my horse. I am young, and I can easily do without it. You have the old one to pull the cart.'

So the young man went to the stable, saddled his horse and trotted off up the road.

He found Thomas finishing his ale at the roadside.

'Have you seen a man on his way to Heaven with a bag of money?' he said.

'What do you want with him, young fellow?' asked Thomas, who was afraid that the man had come to get the money back.

'My mother gave him the money for my old father in Heaven,' answered the young man, 'and I would like to send him my greetings and this horse. Perhaps he has need of one where he is.'

'Indeed he has!' exclaimed Thomas, hardly able to believe his ears. 'You are in luck, young fellow, for it is I who am just off to Heaven with the money. I was refreshing myself with a mug of ale before setting off on my journey. I will gladly ride your horse to Heaven and give it to your father.'

'That is very kind of you,' said the young man, and helped the farmer to mount his horse.

As this very simple young man set off to walk home, the farmer trotted happily back to his wife on the fine horse he had just been given.

'Such people are too simple to have money and horses,' he said to himself.

When he got home, he stabled the horse beside the cow, and went in to tell his wife what had happened.

'Here's forty pounds and a fine young horse,' he said, 'and the owners begged me to take them! I declare,

Martha, I thought you were stupid, but I've found a couple far stupider than you could ever be. Just how simple *can* people be?'

The Witch's Castle

THE wood was dark and thick. It was not safe to go there towards nightfall, for evil things happened. In the middle of the wood was an ancient, stern castle, grey and frowning. In it lived a witch, an old woman with hard, wicked eyes, a wrinkled skin, and hands like claws. All who saw her were afraid. Even the animals shrank from her. But few saw her in daylight, for every morning she would turn herself into an owl or a cat – a lean and cruel cat with green eyes and sharp claws. She would roam through the forest catching little creatures to kill and cook for supper in the evening, when she turned herself back into a witch.

The witch had enchanted the ground about her castle, so that if anyone came within a hundred steps of it they were made to stand quite still until she gave them leave to move once more. The only creatures she allowed within this magic circle were young girls. If any came into the circle she turned them into birds and fastened them up in cages of basket-work. These she kept in a cold, dark room in the castle, never allowing them to see the light of day. She had more than a thousand of these cages, each with its sad little wood-pigeon, canary or nightingale.

One sunny day in spring two people walked in the forest, not far from the witch's castle. One was a sweet girl named Rosamund, as young and beautiful a maiden as had ever lived in that country. Her friend was a young man called Godfrey. He was tall, straight and handsome. They were happy, for Godfrey had asked Rosamund to marry him, and this she had promised to do if her parents agreed. Neither had any doubt that their parents would be pleased, for hers were fond of Godfrey, and Godfrey's parents loved Rosamund. For hours the two lovers walked in the wood, and forgot about the passing of time. Before long the sun had almost gone down behind the trees.

'We must go home,' Godfrey said. 'It is late, and we must not get lost, or we may wander near the witch's castle.'

At this Rosamund shuddered, for everyone knew of the witch and her evil ways.

But sad to tell, the two young people lost their path, and as evening fell they sat down for a while under a tree, because Rosamund was weary. Above her in the branches she heard a wood-pigeon crooning sadly to itself.

Rosamund too began to sing softly, and as Godfrey listened, he also became sad. It seemed as if all their happiness was over. All at once he turned and looked through the trees and, as he did so, he became cold with fear. There, for the first time, he noticed the frowning walls of the witch's castle, and knew that danger was near. He was about to seize Rosamund by the hand and escape with her from the danger, when the little song she was singing suddenly turned into the notes of a nightingale. He was too late. Rosamund was not there. Instead, upon a branch of the tree under which she had been singing, sat a little brown bird, and a great screech-owl was circling round it, crying 'Tu-whit, tu-whit, tu-whoo!' Rosamund had been changed into a nightingale.

At the same moment Godfrey too fell under the witch's spell. He found himself unable to move. He could not even call out the name of Rosamund. The screech-owl vanished into the thicket just as the sun faded behind the trees. Almost immediately a hideous old woman appeared and beckoned to the nightingale to come down from its branch. The witch had a basketwork cage in her

hand. Into this she put the nightingale, clapping the cage-door shut. The bird was her prisoner. She took it away and placed the cage in the cold dark room in the castle. Then she returned to where Godfrey stood, still helpless, as if rooted to the place where he had last seen Rosamund.

The witch spoke to him in her cruel, hard voice, telling him he might go on condition that he left the castle as fast as possible and never came near it again.

At last Godfrey found his voice. 'Give me back the maiden I love,' he begged. 'At least let me see Rosamund and speak to her once more.'

'You shall never see her again, young man. Now go – and remember, get away from here as fast as you can, or you will be turned to stone.'

Godfrey had nothing to do but to obey. Stumbling through the darkness, he made off as fast as he could, determined to begin his search for Rosamund on the morrow.

For many days he looked for someone who might help him in his search, but all were terrified at the very thought of the witch and her enchantments. For weeks he strayed here and there, until one night he sank down to sleep at the edge of a meadow, overcome with weariness and despair. His sleep was restless and troubled. Towards morning he had a dream. He dreamed that he saw growing on a hillside a single blood-red flower with a great pearl in its centre. He stooped and picked the flower and went away with it. Then his dream faded, and he awoke. Somehow he knew that he must find this flower, for it alone could help him to recover the maiden he loved.

So for many days Godfrey went about the countryside, asking everyone he met if they had seen a blood-red flower, growing by itself. No one could help him, and many thought the young man was mad.

Then one day, just as he was beginning to lose hope, the morning sun revealed to him, on a far hillside, something that glowed and sparkled in the grass. He ran towards it, and when he was near enough to see it clearly, he knew that it was what he was looking for – a single blood-red flower with a great drop of dew in the centre, sparkling like a pearl in the sunlight.

The young man picked the flower with trembling hands. Then began the long journey back to the castle. For days he travelled over field and moor, across rivers, through forests, never losing the flower which he believed would bring him happiness.

When he was a hundred steps from the castle, Godfrey was delighted to find that the witch's spells had no power over him. He moved as easily within the magic circle as outside it. He strode up to the great doorway and touched it with the flower. Instantly it flew open. In the courtyard he stood and listened for the singing of birds. He entered an inner door and began to explore the cold and dismal corridors of the castle. At last he heard the sound

he had been listening for – the chirping and singing of hundreds of birds. The sound led him to the dark room where the old woman kept her cages. As he entered the room, she was feeding the birds, pushing scraps of crust and seeds between the bars for her hungry prisoners.

At first the witch did not hear Godfrey approach because of the noise of the birds. When she saw him she was seized with anger. She cursed and stormed at the young man, but she had no power over him. She sprang at him with her bony claws, but she could not come within two steps of him. The flower he held had power to break all her enchantments.

The next thing to be done was to find the cage containing his beloved nightingale. He searched high and low, but there were hundreds of nightingales. All at once, Godfrey saw the old woman craftily creeping away with a cage in her hand. Something told him that this must be the cage he had been seeking. Just as the witch reached the door, Godfrey leaped towards her and touched both the old woman and the cage with the scarlet flower. Instantly she lost her power of enchantment. She screamed horribly, and cursed the young man, but he took no notice, and the witch ran from the room and was seen no more.

At the touch of the flower, the basket-work cage had sprung open and the nightingale was free. With a glad burst of song it was turned instantly into the fair maiden

whom Godfrey had sought so long. It was his own Rosamund. As she clung to him, her arms fast round his neck, they saw that all the other cages had opened and the birds flown out. They too were turned into young and lovely maidens, so that all the witch's evil was undone.

The young man and his betrothed lost no time in getting as far away from the frowning castle as possible. When they returned home, their parents were overjoyed to see them, and preparations were made for the marriage. Rosamund and Godfrey lived happily for the rest of their long lives, and never feared the enchanted castle again.

Poor Fish

A DOCTOR was sitting at dinner one day when his servant came in and told him that a poor villager had come with a cart full of wood. He had unloaded it in the shed at the end of the yard, and was now waiting to be paid.

'Send him in,' ordered the doctor, and the poor carter, removing his hat, stepped into the dining-room.

'How much do I owe you?' asked the doctor.

'One guinea, if you please, sir,' answered the man.

The doctor gave him the money and then poured out a glass of wine.

'Here,' he said, 'you look thirsty. Drink this.'

The man took the wine gladly, and when he had drunk it, he stood looking at the doctor as he sat at dinner.

How fine to be a doctor and live like this, he thought. I wonder if I could learn to be a doctor.

So he told the doctor what was in his mind, and the doctor said, 'I'll tell you what to do. First, sell your horse and cart, and buy a black gown and wig like mine. Next, have a plate with your name printed on it to hang up outside your door. What *is* your name?'

'My name is Fish,' said the poor man.

'That will never do,' said the doctor. 'You must call

yourself "Doctor Knowall". Have that name painted on a sign. You'll find people will come along fast enough.'

So poor Fish thanked the doctor and went off and did as he had been told. He sold his horse and cart and bought a doctor's gown and wig. Then he had a sign hung up outside his house saying:

DOCTOR KNOWALL

Everyone who came that way thought he must be a very wise man indeed.

He had not long set up as a doctor before a splendid coach stopped at his door. It had a coat of arms in gold letters on the side of it, for it belonged to a rich Count. Out of the coach stepped the Count's steward.

'If you are the great Doctor Knowall,' he said, 'get into this coach, for the Count wants you to have dinner with him. He lost a large sum of money and it is believed to be stolen. He commands you to find out who stole it. He thinks it is one of the servants, but he has so many that he can't tell which is the thief. Hurry up, for my master is waiting.'

Now Fish had a wife called Meg, and when she heard where her husband was going, she decided to go with him. She too wanted to dine at the Count's table and to look at his palace. So Fish told the steward he would come if he might bring his wife.

'Very good,' said the steward, 'only hurry, for my master is very anxious to know who the thief is.'

On the way Meg asked her husband what the palace would be like.

'How should I know?' answered Fish. 'One thing is certain, though: there will be a great many servants. I shouldn't wonder if there are three or four of them to serve dinner.'

'Get along with you,' answered Meg. 'I don't believe a word of it.'

'Well, we shall see,' answered Fish.

Before long they reached the Count's palace, and at once they were made to sit down with the Count at his table, and dinner was served. Now the money had indeed been stolen, not by one of the servants but by several. They had taken it, and hidden it under a stone in the yard, meaning to share it among themselves as soon as they got the chance. One of the thieves had been told by the Count's coachman that a great doctor, a very wise man who knew everything, had been sent for to discover who had stolen the money. So they were very nervous.

Well, the meal was begun, and as the first dish was brought in by one of the servants, Fish turned to his wife and said, 'There! That's the first of them.'

Of course he only meant that it was the first of the servants he had told her about in the coach; but the servant overheard him and thought he meant 'the first of the thieves'. This upset him very badly, for he was indeed one of those who had stolen the money.

He went out and told his fellows, so that when it was the second one's turn to bring in a dish, this servant didn't want to go in. But they made him, and when he set down his dish on the table, Fish said to Meg, 'And that's the second of them.'

The second servant was sure that the great Doctor Knowall had guessed the truth, and when he told his fellows what had been said, the third servant was even more unwilling to enter the dining-hall. You can imagine his terror when, as soon as he set down his dish upon the table, Fish turned to his wife and muttered, 'There you are, my dear, that's the third of them!'

When the fourth servant came in with a covered dish, the Count turned to Doctor Knowall and said, 'After dinner, Doctor, I shall ask you to tell me who has stolen my money. But first let us see how clever you are. Since you know everything, tell me what is under that silver dish-cover.'

The poor man had not the slightest idea. How was he to guess what was under the cover? So thinking he would be ruined, he could not help saying to his wife, 'Alas, poor Fish!'

The Count ordered the servant to raise the cover, and there – sure enough – lay a fine fish, steaming in rich sauce.

'Congratulations, Doctor Knowall!' said the Count. 'Now I am sure you'll be able to tell me what I want to know.'

When the fourth servant got back to the kitchen where the other thieves waited, he was trembling with fright.

'He knows everything.' said the servant. 'We had better have a word with him, and try to stop him giving us away.'

So one of them went to the door of the dining-hall and signed to Doctor Knowall to come and have a word with them. They told him that, if he would promise not to give them away, they would show him where the money was hidden. They would give him a reward out of their own savings, but if he told the Count who they were, they would all be hanged and the Doctor would not get so great a reward. Fish agreed to do what they asked, so they showed him the stone in the yard where the money was hidden.

After dinner Fish told the Count that he wasn't able to name the thieves, but he could tell him where to find his money. The Count then followed him into the yard, and under the stone they found nearly all the missing money. He was so grateful that he gave Fish a handsome reward, thanked him, and bade him good-bye. Then the thieving servants also gave him money for not having given them away. So Fish and his wife Meg went back home well satisfied and, with all the money they had been given, managed to live for a long while in ease and comfort.

The Three Clever Sons

THERE was once a man called Simon. He was very old, and his wife had died long ago. But he had three sons – Joseph, Adam and John. Old Simon had a house, but nothing else in the world. Now the three sons were good sons and good brothers, fond of each other and of their father. They were fond, too, of their father's house, and each hoped he would inherit it when Simon died. This troubled the old man.

'I might sell the house, so that you could share the money it brings,' he said. 'But it belonged to my family, and we have had it for hundreds of years. It would be a pity to sell it.'

He thought long and hard about the question of who should inherit the house. At last he had an idea. So he gathered his sons around him, and said, 'Joseph, Adam and John, go out into the world and learn a trade, each of you. The one that becomes most skilled in his trade – to him will I leave our house when I die.'

They readily agreed to the plan, and soon they set out to see which of them would become the best at his trade.

Joseph became apprenticed to a blacksmith, Adam to a barber, and John decided to become a master of fencing.

Joseph worked hard with his hands and at last became a very skilled blacksmith, so skilled that he was appointed to shoe the king's horses. There was no higher post for a blacksmith in all the land. Joseph could take off a worn shoe in a moment, cast another one on his anvil, and hammer it on to the horse's hoof in next to no time. The shoe fitted snugly, and never gave horse or rider trouble until it was worn right down and ready to be replaced. Everyone agreed that never in their lives had they seen such a blacksmith.

All this time Adam was learning to be the best barber in the country. He soon took up employment with the most fashionable hairdresser in town and his services were demanded by all the most important men at court.

He could shave a man smoothly and quickly in a very few minutes, and cut hair to perfection, even for a busy minister of state who had little time to spare for the barber. Everyone agreed that never in their lives had they known a barber more skilled and speedy than Adam.

Nor was John, the youngest, idle. Day and night he practised swordsmanship with the best masters in town. Before long he became one of the most skilful fencers in the land, twisting and twirling his weapon until you imagined he had been born and brought up with a sword in his hand. Never had anyone seen such a bold, skilful and resourceful fencer in his life. People came from far and near to watch John, the young swordsman, as he engaged in fencing displays against the most seasoned opponents in all the land.

So at length the three brothers went home to their father to tell him how they had fared. He was delighted to see them, and as it was a fine sunny day, they sat together on a bench outside the house and talked about their skill and prospects.

'We must think how to decide which of you is the cleverest,' said old Simon.

Just at that moment they caught sight of a hare running across the meadow towards them.

'This is my chance,' said Adam the barber.

So saying, he seized his shaving bowl and brushed up a fine, soapy lather in no time. Then he picked up his razor with one hand and grasped the hare in the other as it leaped towards him.

'Swish-swosh' went the soapy brush, and 'snip-snap' went the razor, gleaming in the sun, and lo and behold! the hare was shaved as clean as a new-laid egg!

'Why, this is miraculous!' exclaimed the old man, clapping his son on the shoulder. 'If your brothers beat you, they must be magicians!'

At this moment along came a gentleman in a coach

drawn by two fine black steeds. 'Clip-clop' they came along the highway.

'This is *my* chance,' cried Joseph the blacksmith.

Seizing a horseshoe, some nails and a hammer, he whipped off one of the horse's shoes in less than no time, and hammered on the new one, so that the horse hardly knew what had happened.

'This is splendid!' cried old Simon. 'Did you ever see such skill in a blacksmith before? I declare, I shouldn't wonder if you were to get the house after all, Joseph.'

They were so busy congratulating Joseph on his skill, that they did not notice a big black cloud that had come up and hidden the sun. Suddenly it began to rain. At once John, the fencer, drew his sword and twirled it about in the air so that not a drop of rain fell on his father's head. Faster and faster fell the rain, and faster and faster flashed the sword, this way and that; and so fast and furiously did John twirl his sword that not a single drop of rain splashed down on old Simon. Presently the shower passed, and the sun came out again. John wiped the raindrops off his sword and snapped it back into the scabbard.

This masterly display had hardly made him lose his breath. Smiling and triumphant, he said, 'There Father! What do you think of that?'

'Why, I can hardly believe it,' said the old man. 'Was ever a father blessed with three such clever sons? I think

you will agree, all of you, that it is John who wins the prize. What do you say?'

The other two were so delighted at their young brother's skill that they at once agreed that he was the winner. It was John who was to have the house when their father died.

Well, in course of time Simon fell ill, and as he was very old and feeble he never recovered. When he died, the brothers agreed that John was to have the house.

'I should not like it here without you,' said John. 'There is room for all of us. Let us all live together in peace and friendship.'

And this is what they did. They lived together in their

father's house, each following his own trade until they all became rich and famous. Everyone who went there agreed that never had there been three such clever brothers who lived in such harmony.

A Story With No End

THE fox was hungry. He was always hungry. Never could he catch enough to satisfy his enormous appetite.

One day he crept out of the wood where he had been trying, in vain, to find a nice plump rabbit for his dinner, when there, right in front of his eyes, what should he see but a row of seven fat geese sitting in the middle of a green field.

'What luck!' said the fox to himself. 'I will eat them all. What a meal they will make!'

He stalked boldly up to the seven fat geese, and said aloud, 'Good morning, my dears! What a fine dinner you will make. It's no good looking anxious, for you can't get away. I shall eat you one by one, beginning with the fattest.'

Then he grinned a wicked grin, showing all his teeth, and licked his lips with his long, red tongue.

The geese were very worried, and began to look the picture of misery. They had no idea what to say to the wicked fox. But at last one of them spoke up boldly and said, 'Mr Fox, we know we cannot get away. You can run much faster than we can. It is clear that we must

die to make your dinner. But first, Mr Fox, will you grant us one favour?'

'What is that?' asked the fox.

'First let us say our prayers. Let us pray to the god of all geese, who lives up in the blue sky. We will beg our god to forgive us our sins, and after that we will die happy. Only think, Mr Fox, if you were going to die, would you not pray to your god to forgive your sins?'

'There is something in what you say,' agreed the fox.

'That is a truly religious thought, and does you credit. If I let you say your prayers, what then?'

'Just as soon as we have finished our prayers,' said the goose, 'you may kill us all, one at a time. We will sit in a row, with the fattest first, so that you may take your pick and eat us all in turn. Only let us say our prayers!'

'Very well,' said the fox, who liked to appear a generous fellow, though everyone knows how wicked he is. 'Begin your prayers now, and I will not touch a feather of your necks till you have finished.'

So immediately the first goose began to pray.

'Gabble-gabble,' it said, 'gabble-gabble-gabble.'

Then the second one looked up into the blue sky and said, 'Gabble-gabble.'

The third one began in the same way. Each one of the seven geese looked up into the sky and began to say its prayers. So they went on, and if one stopped to take breath, another started.

And if the geese had ever stopped saying their prayers, this story might have had an end. But to tell you the truth, those geese have never stopped gabbling yet . . .

Perhaps they never will.

also by James Reeves

The Merry-Go-Round

An unrivalled collection of verse – poems, folk rhymes and songs, carols, nonsense songs, story poems, lyrics and ballads – each one especially chosen to give delight, whether it is an old favourite or something completely new and unusual. Poems to make you laugh, riddles to guess, songs to sing, the very best from every kind of poetry, arranged here in a lively sequence with nothing dull or dreary to spoil the sparkling whole.

There are poems for six year olds, and many for twelve year olds; most readers over nine will love them all.

This Puffin edition contains a few less than the 400 poems of the original edition, and most of the other poems you can already find in the other Puffin poetry books.

Some other Young Puffins for 5 and 6 year olds

DORRIE AND THE BIRTHDAY EGGS
DORRIE AND THE HAUNTED HOUSE
DORRIE AND THE GOBLIN
DORRIE AND THE WIZARD'S SPELL

Patricia Coombs

A series of delightful books about the little witch, Dorrie, her cat Gink, and her mother The Big Witch. They all live cheerfully together in a house with a tower and have many exciting adventures.

PROFESSOR BRANESTAWM'S POCKET MOTOR CAR
and
PROFESSOR BRANESTAWM AND THE WILD LETTERS

Norman Hunter

Two great bits of Branestawm battiness. This time, Professor Branestawm has invented an inflatable car as an answer to Pagwell's parking problem and a letter-writing machine for everyone who hates letter-writing.

THE OWL WHO WAS AFRAID OF THE DARK

Jill Tomlinson

In this warm and endearing book Plop, the baby barn-owl, conquers his fear of the dark with the help of some interesting and unusual people and a wise, mysterious cat.

DINNER AT ALBERTA'S

Russell Hoban

Arthur the crocodile has extremely bad manners – until he is invited to Alberta's for dinner.

THE NEW RED BIKE

Simon Watson

Sixteen short stories about a lively and logical small boy called Wallace, his nice parents, his daily adventures and occasional disgraces, all told with humour and understanding.

HIDE TILL DAYTIME

Joan Phipson

The two children had been locked into the big department store by mistake at closing time, and whose were those prowling steps they could hear through the dark?

THE WORST WITCH
THE WORST WITCH STRIKES AGAIN

Jill Murphy

Mildred Hubble is the most disastrous dunce of all at Miss Cackle's training school for witches. But even the worst witch scores the occasional triumph!

MRS PEPPERPOT'S YEAR

Alf Prøysen

'Goodness,' said the little girl in hospital when she saw that the nice old lady who was tucking her in had suddenly shrunk to a few inches high, 'you must be Mrs Pepperpot!' 'Right first time,' said Mrs Pepperpot, 'and now it's your turn to help me.'

MATTHEW'S SECRET SURPRISES

Teresa Verschoyle

Happy stories about a little boy exploring his new home, a cottage tucked away by the sea, with all its secrets and surprises.
(Original)

CARROT TOPS

Joan Wyatt

Fifteen stories of everyday events like making a jelly, growing a carrot-top garden, visiting Granny – all tinged with the make-believe that young children love.

CLEVER POLLY AND THE STUPID WOLF
POLLY AND THE WOLF AGAIN
TALES OF POLLY AND THE HUNGRY WOLF

Catherine Storr

The wolf had been hanging round Polly's house for ages trying to catch her and eat her up, but Polly was *much* too clever to be caught by all his tricks and disguises.

Who is he?

His name is Smudge, and he's the mascot of the Junior Puffin Club.

What is that?

It's a Club for children between 4 and 8 who are beginning to discover and enjoy books for themselves.

How does it work?

On joining, members are sent a Club badge and Membership Card, a sheet of stickers, and their first copy of the magazine, *The Egg*, which is sent to them four times a year. As well as stories, pictures, puzzles and things to make, there are competitions to enter and, of course, news about new Puffins.

For details of cost and an application form, send a stamped addressed envelope to: